P9-DCJ-095

HOCKEY SUPERSTARS

Paul Romanuk

ALL-TIME GREATS! VOL. 1

Scholastic Canada Ltd.
Toronto New York London Auckland Sydney
Mexico City New Delhi Hong Kong Buenos Aires

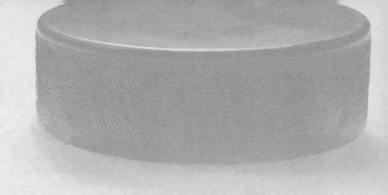

J. Leary/Bruce Bennett/Getty Images: Cover
Art Rickerby//Time Life Pictures/Getty Images: Hull (inset)
Bill Eppridge//Time Life Pictures/Getty Images: Hull
Bruce Bennett/Getty Images: Dryden, Gretzky, Harvey (inset),
Howe (inset), Lafleur, Lemieux, Potvin
Doug MacLellan/Hockey Hall of Fame: all awards
George Silk//Time Life Pictures/Getty Images: Plante
Graphic Artists/Hockey Hall of Fame: Béliveau
Hockey Hall of Fame: Howe, Morenz (inset)
Hulton Archive/Getty Images: Béliveau (inset)
Imperial Oil-Turofsky/Hockey Hall of Fame: Apps, Harvey, Plante (inset), Richard (all images)
James Rice/Hockey Hall of Fame: Morenz
Ken Levine/Allsport: Roy
London Life-Portnoy/Hockey Hall of Fame: Sittler
Melchior DiGiacomo/Getty Images: Esposito, Orr
Miles Nadal/Hockey Hall of Fame: Gretzky (with trophies)
O-Pee-Chee/Hockey Hall of Fame: Bossy
Robert Laberge/Allsport: Bourque
Todd Warshaw/Allsport: Coffey

Library and Archives Canada Cataloguing in Publication
Romanuk, Paul
Hockey superstars : all-time greats! / Paul Romanuk.

ISBN 978-1-4431-0736-5 (v. 1).--ISBN 978-1-4431-0712-9 (v. 2)

1. Hockey players--Biography--Juvenile literature. 2. National
Hockey League--Biography--Juvenile literature. I. Title.

GV848.5.A1R652 2011   j796.962092'2   C2011-902076-9

Text copyright © 2005, 2011 by Paul Romanuk.
All rights reserved.

No part of this publication may be reproduced or stored in a retrieval system, or
transmitted in any form or by any means, electronic, mechanical, recording, or otherwise,
without written permission of the publisher, Scholastic Canada Ltd., 604 King Street West,
Toronto, Ontario M5V 1E1, Canada. In the case of photocopying or other reprographic
copying, a licence must be obtained from Access Copyright (Canadian Copyright Licensing
Agency), 1 Yonge Street, Suite 800, Toronto, Ontario M5V 1E5 (1-800-893-5777).

6 5 4 3 2 1   Printed in Singapore   46   11 12 13 14

INTRODUCTION

My "Golden Age of Sports" was in the 1970s with players like Guy Lafleur, Phil Esposito, Ken Dryden and Darryl Sittler, just to name a few. I think the golden age of sports is probably when you are between the ages of 9 and 16, give or take a couple of years. Those are wonderful and amazing years for sports fans. Those are years when you are developing both an understanding and a love of the game — whatever it is. You have the time and the passion to live, sleep, eat and breathe the games. For me, it was hockey. If I wasn't playing it, I was reading about it. I read EVERYTHING about hockey — magazines, newspapers and especially the backs of the hundreds of hockey cards I collected. I filled scrapbooks with pictures and stories of my favorite players and teams. I cried when they lost and celebrated when they won. It was my world.

I hope, if this is your golden age of sports, that in the future you'll enjoy reading stories about hall-of-fame greats like Sidney Crosby, Alex Ovechkin, the Sedins or whoever your favorite player is. I know I had a great time writing about so many of my old heroes — true all-time greats.

Paul.

SYL APPS

What can be said about Syl Apps? He was one of the greatest hockey players ever to play the game. He had a great shot, played hard but fair (he finished his entire career with only 56 penalty minutes) and was regarded as one of the great on- and off-ice leaders of his era.

Syl was an outstanding, multi-talented athlete. He was discovered by Toronto Maple Leafs' general manager Conn Smythe, who went to watch him play football at McMaster University in Hamilton, Ontario, where he was working toward a degree in economics. Smythe was so impressed with his athleticism that he offered him a hockey contract right then and there. But Syl passed on the offer because he was scheduled to compete for Canada in the pole vault in the 1936 Berlin Olympics. Smythe wasn't happy about having to wait but felt that Syl would be worth it.

"There have been many remarkable athletes in Canadian sport, but few have been more outstanding. There is only one Apps."

— *The Hamilton Spectator*, April 24, 1948, after Apps announced his retirement

---

And he was. Syl started his NHL career in 1936–1937 with the Leafs and won the Calder Trophy for Rookie of the Year — he led the league in assists with 29, and finished second in league scoring with 45 points. Although the next season he was put on a line with two other outstanding players — Bob Davidson and Gord Drillon — for three years in a row, the team failed to win a championship.

Syl finally won a Cup with the Leafs in 1942 in one of the most dramatic final series ever. The powerful Detroit Red Wings took a 3–0 lead in the series and Toronto looked defeated. But, led by their captain, Syl, the Leafs came back to win the next four games and the Cup. It is the only time in NHL history a team has come back from a 3–0 deficit in the final.

In 1943 Syl left the Leafs for the next two seasons to serve in the Canadian Army during the Second World War. He returned to the Leafs in 1945 and set career highs in goals for the next three seasons. He led Toronto to Stanley Cup Championships in 1947 and 1948 before retiring. He was only 33, and at the top of his game. He is the only athlete to be honored by the Hockey Hall of Fame, the Canadian Sports Hall of Fame and the Canadian Amateur Athletics Hall of Fame. Syl was not only an outstanding hockey player, but all-around athlete.

Did You Know?
The year Syl won the Lady Byng Trophy as "the player adjudged to have exhibited the best type of sportsmanship and gentlemanly conduct combined with a high standard of playing ability," he did not take a single penalty.

		GP	G	A	PTS	PIM
CAREER STATS	**Totals 1936–1937 to 1947–1948** **(missed 1943–1944 and 1944–1945 serving in the military)**					
	Regular Season	423	201	231	432	56
	Playoffs	69	25	29	54	8
	Major Awards	Stanley Cup: 1942, 1947, 1948				
		Calder Trophy: 1937				
		Lady Byng Trophy: 1942				

Born: January 18, 1915, in Paris, Ontario
Died: December 24, 1998
Position: Center
Height: 1.83 m (6')
Weight: 84 kg (185 lbs.)
NHL Team: Toronto Maple Leafs

JEAN BÉLIVEAU

He was called "Le Gros Bill" and he was a massive presence in one of the greatest dynasties in the history of sports. Jean Béliveau was big — 1.90 meters, 93 kilograms — at a time when the average NHL player was only 1.78 meters, 82 kilograms. But it wasn't only his size that made him a legend: Jean was the captain of the Montreal Canadiens from 1961 until he retired in 1971 and was part of ten Stanley Cup wins during his 18 seasons with the team. Imagine that — ten Stanley Cup rings! And he was the number one center on a team that won an NHL record five Cups in a row from 1956 to 1960.

> **"Ever since I was a young boy, I had dreamed about two things. One was to wear the sweater of the Montreal Canadiens; the other was to win the Stanley Cup. I have been a lucky man to realize both of those dreams during my life."**

Not only was Jean a great skater, passer and playmaker, but he was also a great team player. His coaches would frequently put younger, less experienced players on his line because they knew they could count on Jean's unselfish style of play to help develop their skills.

"I always believed that as captain of the Montreal Canadiens, you had to help the team to develop young players. I would tell the younger guys, 'I'm the veteran of the line; things will be fine. You just play your game,'" he once said.

It was that kind of approach that made Jean such a valuable part of Montreal's success, right up until his final season.

At the end of the 1969–1970 season he approached Montreal general manager Sam Pollock and told him he wanted to retire. Almost 40 years old, Jean didn't feel that he could contribute the way he once had. But Pollock knew that his team needed a veteran leader. Jean decided to stay on one more season. His leadership once again brought the Canadiens all the way to the championship. They won the Cup on the road that year, in Chicago. As he accepted the Cup and skated around the ice, fans stood and cheered. A few had tears in their eyes. Most likely they knew they were watching the final bow in the career of one of the greatest players ever to play the game.

Did You Know?

In 1994 the Government of Canada asked Jean if he would consider becoming the country's Governor General. He turned down the offer. He thought it was more important to spend time with his family.

Born: August 31, 1931,
in Trois Rivieres, Quebec
Position: Center
Height: 1.90 m (6'3")
Weight: 93 kg (205 lbs.)
NHL Team: Montreal Canadiens

CAREER STATS

Totals 1953–1954 to 1970–1971

	GP	G	A	PTS	PIM
Regular Season	1125	507	712	1219	1029
Playoffs	162	79	97	176	211

Major Awards Stanley Cup: 1956, 1957, 1958, 1959, 1960, 1965, 1966, 1968, 1969, 1971
Hart Trophy: 1956, 1964
Art Ross Trophy: 1956
Conn Smythe Trophy: 1965

MIKE BOSSY

Mike Bossy was a champion goal scorer. He had 573 goals in only 752 career games, and he managed to score 50 or more for nine seasons in a row — a record that no other player has ever been able to match.

Like the great Phil Esposito before him, Mike was a natural at finding the "sweet spot" around the net. Time and again he would come out in the right place at the right time. That, and his great one-timers, made him one of the most dangerous offensive players ever.

"It was an amazing time . . . it was an unbelievable feeling playing for as great a team as I played for."

Mike grew up in Montreal, one of the great hockey cities of the world. By the time he was 15, Mike was playing for the Laval Nationale, a local junior team. There, he scored over 300 goals in four seasons. But he was seen as a player who wasn't physical enough to be in the NHL. Despite being an incredible junior player, Mike was the 15th pick in the 1977 Amateur Draft when the New York Islanders chose him. Mike blazed through his first season, scoring 53 goals (an NHL record at the time) and winning the Calder Trophy as Rookie of the Year. He was teamed with great playmaker Bryan Trottier and big, physical winger Clark Gillies, and the three formed one of the dominant NHL lines of the late 1970s and early 1980s.

"You are never sure how a situation will turn out," recalled Mike years later, "but once I got to New York and saw the kind of guys I was playing with and the potential for that group, I really didn't look at any level as being unattainable."

Mike played his entire career with the Islanders and shared in four consecutive Stanley Cup Championships. In 1980–1981 he scored 50 goals in 50 games, tying a record set by Maurice "Rocket" Richard that had lasted 36 years. He was an All-Star eight times. Mike only had 210 penalty minutes his entire career, and received the Lady Byng Trophy as the NHL's Most Gentlemanly Player three times.

Unfortunately, Mike was forced into retirement after suffering from chronic back pain at the age of 30 in 1987. In 1991 he was inducted into the Hockey Hall of Fame.

Did You Know?
Mike scored the Stanley Cup winning goal for the Islanders in both 1982 and 1983. He was also named the playoff MVP in 1982.

Born: January 22, 1957, in Montreal, Quebec
Position: Right Wing
Height: 1.83 m (6')
Weight: 84 kg (186 lbs.)
NHL Team: New York Islanders

CAREER STATS

Totals 1977–1978 to 1986–1987

	GP	G	A	PTS	PIM
Regular Season	752	573	553	1126	210
Playoffs	129	85	75	160	38

Major Awards	Stanley Cup: 1980, 1981, 1982, 1983
	Calder Trophy: 1978
	Conn Smythe Trophy: 1982
	Lady Byng Trophy: 1983, 1984, 1986

RAY BOURQUE

Even before Ray Bourque had achieved his career goal of being part of a Stanley Cup Championship team, his place as one of the great men in hockey history was assured.

Ray exploded onto the scene in 1979 when he was the Boston Bruins' first pick in the NHL Entry Draft. In his first season he won the Calder Trophy after earning an impressive 65 points — at the time, a record for a rookie defenseman.

Most hockey fans expected Ray to finish his career in Boston. But with his career coming to an end, he longed to win a Stanley Cup — something that he hadn't yet done with Boston.

"Besides actually playing the game, the most fun of being a hockey player is being part of a team. Being in the room with guys pursuing a shared goal."

In March 2000 Ray let Boston general manager Harry Sinden know that he wanted to play for a team that had a chance to win a Cup. So he was traded to the Colorado Avalanche, a team that had a great shot at winning the Cup that season. When he retired two years later, Ray talked about how much he owed the Boston organization.

"I will always be a Bruin in my heart and I have to thank Harry Sinden for giving me my first chance in Boston and the chance in Colorado [with the trade] to win a Cup."

But there was no championship for Ray that year. At the start of the playoffs the following year, he handed out baseball caps crested with "Mission 16W" to all of his Colorado teammates. Sixteen — the number of playoff games it takes to win a Stanley Cup Championship. And that year, he reached his dream.

"I remember in the final game I couldn't breathe in the last 30 seconds," recalled Ray, "and it wasn't because I was tired. It was just too much with all the emotions."

As Ray held hockey's greatest prize high over his head, fans knew then that they were witnessing the end of an era. A few weeks later, he announced his retirement.

Ray left the game as the highest scoring defenseman ever — 1,579 points in 1,612 regular season games. He was named an NHL All-Star an astounding 19 times. But the career number that means the most to him is one: one Stanley Cup Championship.

Did You Know?

Ray wore the number 7 for the first eight seasons of his career. He volunteered to switch to 77 when the Bruins wanted to honor Phil Esposito by retiring his old number.

Born: December 28, 1960, in Montreal, Quebec
Position: Defense
Height: 1.80 m (5'11")
Weight: 99 kg (219 lbs.)
NHL Teams: Boston Bruins, Colorado Avalanche

CAREER STATS

Totals 1979–1980 to 2000–2001

	GP	G	A	PTS	PIM
Regular Season	1612	410	1169	1579	1141
Playoffs	214	41	139	180	171

Major Awards	Stanley Cup: 2001
	Calder Trophy: 1980
	Norris Trophy: 1987, 1988, 1990, 1991, 1994

PAUL COFFEY

During his prime with the Edmonton Oilers, Paul Coffey always seemed to have the puck. His acceleration was explosive. He could change direction and speed at will — and he made it look easy.

"People used to say I was a natural. Nobody's a natural," said Paul. "You work hard to get good and then work to get better. It's hard to stay on top."

During the early 1980s, with players like Coffey, Wayne Gretzky, Jari Kurri and Mark Messier, the Oilers struck fear into many a team. Their spectacular combination of speed, passing and shooting made the team seem almost invincible. Paul played a vital role in the first three championships the Oilers won during the 1980s and 1990s. He also won back-to-back Norris Trophies in 1985 and 1986 as the best defenseman in the league.

"When we've got the puck, they can't score."

"When I look back at my career, those Edmonton years stand out," recalled Paul. "When we beat the Islanders and won our first Stanley Cup it was really special. We had a great group of guys and it all just clicked."

Paul was traded to Pittsburgh just before the 1987–1988 season and was part of his fourth Stanley Cup Championship in 1991. While he was in Pittsburgh, Paul had the chance to play with superstar Mario Lemieux. Imagine a career where you had the chance to play with two of the greatest offensive players in the history of the game — Lemieux and Gretzky.

"You can't really compare the two," said Paul while he was in Pittsburgh. "All I will say is that I'd rather be playing with them than against them."

Paul was eventually traded to Los Angeles in 1992 and then to Detroit in 1993. With the Red Wings in 1995, he won the Norris Trophy for the third and final time of his career.

Paul was named an NHL All-Star eight times and finished his career as the second-highest scoring defenseman in NHL history. In 2004 Paul's outstanding achievements were recognized when, in his first year of eligibility, he was voted into the Hockey Hall of Fame.

Did You Know?

Although he was the 6th player taken in the 1980 Entry Draft, Paul was the 4th defenseman chosen. He was drafted after Dave Babych, Larry Murphy and Darren Veitch.

Born: June 1, 1961, in Weston, Ontario
Position: Defense
Height: 1.83 m (6')
Weight: 8 kg (190 lbs.)
NHL Teams: Edmonton Oilers, Pittsburgh Penguins, Los Angeles Kings, Detroit Red Wings, Hartford Whalers, Philadelphia Flyers, Chicago Blackhawks, Carolina Hurricanes, Boston Bruins

CAREER STATS

Totals 1980–1981 to 2000–2001

	GP	G	A	PTS	PIM
Regular Season	1409	396	1135	1531	1802
Playoffs	194	59	137	196	264

Major Awards	Stanley Cup: 1984, 1985, 1987, 1991
	Norris Trophy: 1985, 1986, 1995

KEN DRYDEN

From his start as a top goaltender in the NHL to his career in politics, Ken Dryden has shown that he's anything but ordinary.

Instead of starting off his career by playing junior hockey, Ken played for Cornell University in the United States. He also played on Canada's National Team from 1968 until 1970.

He started his professional career with Montreal's minor league team in Halifax in 1970–1971 and the Canadiens called him up later that season.

"Because the demands on a goalie are mostly mental, it means that for a goalie, the biggest enemy is himself. Not a puck, not an opponent, not a quirk of size or style. Him."

During the first round of the 1970–1971 playoffs, Montreal faced the Boston Bruins — a team with stars like Phil Esposito and Bobby Orr. Ken had only played six games that season, but coach Al MacNeil decided that he would start him against the Bruins. Mainly because of Ken's spectacular goaltending, the Canadiens forced the Bruins to a seventh game. Ken stunned the Bruins with a stellar performance and Montreal won the game 4–2.

"I can't believe that giraffe stopped me so many times," said an exasperated Esposito after the series was over.

Montreal went on to win the Stanley Cup that year — the first of six Cups that Ken would be a part of during his goaltending career. Ken was named the Conn Smythe Trophy winner as the Most Valuable Player of the playoffs. He followed that by winning the Calder Trophy the following season. Because Ken had played so few regular-season games in 1970–1971, he was still considered a rookie for the 1971–1972 season. It was the first time in the history of the NHL that a player had been named the playoff MVP before becoming Rookie of the Year.

In September 1972 Ken played for Team Canada against the Soviet Union in the now legendary eight-game Summit Series. Ken was in goal for the deciding game and backstopped Canada to a dramatic 6–5 win.

"Nothing in hockey ever brought me so low or took me so high," said Ken reflecting on the series. "And nothing ever meant as much to me as that experience."

Ken retired after the 1978–1979 season, at the age of 32. Since then he's worked as a television broadcaster, a writer, President of the Toronto Maple Leafs and also as a Member of the Canadian Parliament. Now, that's extraordinary.

Did You Know?

Ken sat out the entire 1973–1974 season as a result of a contract dispute with the Montreal Canadiens. While he was sitting out, he worked for a law firm in Toronto, completing his law degree.

Born: August 8, 1947, in Hamilton, Ontario
Position: Goaltender
Height: 1.93 m (6'4")
Weight: 93 kg (205 lbs.)
NHL Team: Montreal Canadiens

CAREER STATS

Totals 1971–1972 to 1978–1979

	GP	W	L	T	SO	GAA
Regular Season	397	258	57	74	46	2.24
Playoffs	112	80	32	—	10	2.40

Major Awards	
Stanley Cup:	1971, 1973, 1976, 1977, 1978, 1979
Calder Trophy:	1972
Conn Smythe Trophy:	1971
Vezina Trophy:	1973, 1976, 1977, 1978, 1979

PHIL ESPOSITO

It was strength, determination and talent that led Phil "Espo" Esposito to become the dominant center of his era in the NHL. Phil had a quick and accurate shot and was a great passer. Before Wayne Gretzky came on the scene in the 1980s, Phil was the greatest scoring center the NHL had ever seen.

Phil started his career with the Chicago Blackhawks in 1964. After three seasons in Chicago, the team seemed to lose patience with his development, so they traded him to the Boston Bruins. Within three years of the trade, the Bruins were Stanley Cup champions, and Phil had grown into one of the game's great leaders. Phil was an outstanding NHL player and went on to win the league scoring title four seasons in a row.

"Play with passion and heart. If you don't have passion and carry it into sports, or any other job, you won't succeed."

But where Phil really made his mark was his amazing scoring and leadership during the 1972 Summit Series between Canada and the Soviet Union. Years later, Phil referred to the Summit Series as "the toughest thing I ever went through in my life as a hockey player."

It was the first time Canada had used NHL players against the great Soviet amateurs, and people expected Canada to dominate the series. They didn't. The team struggled through the first four games of the series with only one win, two losses and a tie. When Canada lost the fourth game in Vancouver 5–3, fans started to boo. Phil was interviewed on national TV right after the game, and millions watched as the captain stood up for his teammates.

"If the Russian fans boo their players in Moscow like you people are booing us, I'll come back and apologize personally to each and every one of you, but I don't think that's going to happen. We're doing our best. They're a good hockey team, and we don't know what we can do better, but we're going to have to figure it out. But to be booed like this is ridiculous."

Canada ended up winning the series in a spectacular final game. There will never be another series quite like it, and it's unlikely that there will ever be another player with the skill and the ability to lead as well as Phil did.

Did You Know?

In 1968–1969 Phil became the first player in NHL history to score 100 points in a season. He finished with 126 points — the first of six 100-point seasons he had during his career.

		Totals 1963–1964 to 1980–1981				
Born: February 20, 1942, in Sault Ste. Marie, Ontario			GP	G	A	PTS	PIM
Position: Center	CAREER STATS	Regular Season	1282	717	873	1590	910
Height: 1.85 m (6'1")		Playoffs	130	61	76	137	138
Weight: 93 kg (205 lbs.)		Major Awards	Stanley Cup: 1970, 1972				
NHL Teams: Chicago Blackhawks, Boston Bruins, New York Rangers			Hart Trophy: 1969, 1974				
			Art Ross Trophy: 1969, 1971, 1972, 1973, 1974				

WAYNE GRETZKY

Wayne Gretzky — "The Great One" — is without a doubt the greatest hockey player of his time. Many would even describe him as the finest player in the game's history.

From an early age, Wayne seemed to be a natural at hockey. He demonstrated skills as early as six years old that led to him playing in leagues with much older players. Despite his small size, his skills increased and he started setting records even then.

"I will never play again. The next time you see me skating will be with my kids."

— Wayne Gretzky at his retirement announcement in 1999

In 1977–1978 Wayne played for the Sault Ste. Marie Greyhounds of the Ontario Hockey Association where he first donned the number 99. In 1978 he turned to professional hockey when he joined the Indianapolis Racers of the World Hockey Association. The team folded shortly after, and Wayne was sold to the Edmonton Oilers.

On October 10, 1979, Wayne played his first NHL game where he earned his first point — an assist. From there his role in hockey history was sealed. He went on to shatter records many thought were unbreakable, like Phil Esposito's record of 76 goals in a season — Wayne scored a stunning 92.

As great a goal-scorer as Wayne was, what set him apart was his remarkable ability to pass the puck. During his years with the Oilers, Wayne accumulated an amazing 1,086 assists.

In 1988, in a shocking move, the Oilers traded Wayne to the Los Angeles Kings. He spent almost eight seasons there before he moved on to the St. Louis Blues and finally to the New York Rangers.

Then, during the 1998–1999 season, Wayne decided it was time to retire. During his final two games, first in Ottawa and then in New York, the hockey world was transfixed as The Great One bid an emotional farewell to his days as a player. When he retired he either held or shared 61 NHL records.

Wayne was general manager for Canada's 2002 gold-winning Men's Olympic Hockey team and Canada's 2004 championship-winning World Cup hockey team. He also was part-owner and coach of the Phoenix Coyotes from 2004–2009

"The biggest thing is that you wish you could still play," said Wayne. "But I've moved on and enjoy the things I'm doing in my life right now."

And fans have enjoyed it as well. Many can't imagine the day when he's no longer involved in the game at all.

Did You Know?

In 1985–1986, when Wayne set an NHL record with 215 points in a season, he had 163 assists. He would have won the NHL scoring title with his assist total alone.

CAREER STATS

Born: January 26, 1961, in Brantford, Ontario
Position: Center
Height: 1.83 m (6')
Weight: 84 kg (185 lbs.)
NHL Teams: Edmonton Oilers, Los Angeles Kings, St. Louis Blues, New York Rangers

Totals 1979–1980 to 1998–1999

	GP	G	A	PTS	PIM
Regular Season	1487	894	1963	2857	577
Playoffs	208	122	260	382	66

Major Awards	
Stanley Cup:	1984, 1985, 1987, 1988
Hart Trophy:	1980, 1981, 1982, 1983, 1984, 1985, 1986, 1987, 1989
Art Ross Trophy:	1981, 1982, 1983, 1984, 1985, 1986, 1987, 1990, 1991, 1994
Conn Smythe Trophy:	1985, 1988
Lady Byng Trophy:	1980, 1991, 1992, 1994, 1999

DOUG HARVEY

Before Bobby Orr came along in the late 1960s, there was no question who was considered the greatest defenseman of all time — the Montreal Canadiens' Doug Harvey. He had the ability to skate fast and play both offensively or defensively. He changed speeds beautifully and made long passes with great accuracy. And he made it look easy. It's no surprise that, with Doug on the blue line, the Montreal Canadiens won an NHL-record five Stanley Cup Championships in a row from 1956 to 1960.

"Setting up my teammates was always more important to me than scoring myself."

An all-around athlete, Doug could have played either professional football or baseball — teams from both sports had made him offers before he decided to go with his first love, hockey. In 1947–1948 Doug made his NHL debut and launched a 14-season career with the Habs. During his years in Montreal, Doug was named the best defenseman in the league seven times and was a huge part of six Stanley Cup Championships.

Although he had a terrific shot, Doug preferred to pass the puck off to an open teammate rather than take the shot himself. He always reasoned that forwards were paid to score, not defensemen. In almost 20 NHL campaigns he never scored more than nine goals in a single season, but his assist totals were always solid.

A conscientious man, Doug always stood up for what he believed in. It was that quality that most likely cost him his job in Montreal. This was a time when team owners made a lot of money and controlled players' careers, and he didn't feel this was right. He felt players should be paid more and not have to pay for things like their own medical expenses. He was one of the first superstars to try to form a players' association. Montreal management was not happy about this and traded Doug to the New York Rangers. There he won the Norris Trophy one more time, but his career was never again as great as it had been in Montreal.

After his career ended, Doug had some difficult times and ended up homeless. When his old team found out, they hired him to work as a scout. Doug died of liver disease in 1989.

Did You Know?

Doug scored the Cup-winning goal in the 1954 final against the Detroit Red Wings — sort of. He actually tipped a clearing attempt by a Detroit player and the puck ended up behind his own goalie, Gerry McNeil.

Born: December 19, 1924, in Montreal, Quebec
Died: December 26, 1989
Position: Defense
Height: 1.80 m (5'11")
Weight: 85 kg (187 lbs.)
NHL Teams: Montreal Canadiens, New York Rangers, St. Louis Blues

CAREER STATS

Totals 1947–1948 to 1968–1969

	GP	G	A	PTS	PIM
Regular Season	1113	88	452	540	1216
Playoffs	137	8	64	72	152

Major Awards	Stanley Cup: 1953, 1956, 1957, 1958, 1959, 1960
	Norris Trophy: 1955, 1956, 1957, 1958, 1960, 1961, 1962

GORDIE HOWE

He did it all. Gordie Howe won Stanley Cup Championships, scoring titles, numerous awards and was the all-time leading scorer in the history of the game when he retired. He even played in the NHL with his two sons.

Gordie was 18 years old when he started his professional hockey career with the Detroit Red Wings in 1946–1947. He had a decent, although unspectacular, rookie season with seven goals and 15 assists.

Back in those days the NHL was a tough place for a first-year player. There were only six teams and, as a result, not many jobs. Veteran opponents would treat rookies harshly, and if you wanted to last in the league, you couldn't back down. Gordie never did.

"It's about loving what you're doing. If you really love what you do, you can overcome any handicap or pain or soreness and keep playing for a long time."

"That's just the way it was back then," said Gordie years later. "You had to prove yourself. If you backed down you were finished."

In his second season, Gordie was put on a line with his friend Ted Lindsay and a veteran center named Sid Abel. They formed what became known as "The Production Line," and they dominated NHL scoring for the next five seasons.

After 25 years with Detroit, and playing with chronic pain in an arthritic left wrist, Gordie retired in 1971. The retirement didn't last long. Two seasons later he returned to professional hockey when he signed to play with the Houston Aeros of the World Hockey Association. Gordie wanted the opportunity to play on the same team as his two sons, Mark and Marty. Later the three moved to play with the New England Whalers for a couple of seasons before the WHA merged with the NHL. Gordie returned to the NHL for one final season with the Whalers. At the age of 51, he played a full season and finished with 41 points before finally retiring for good. Final total: 1,767 NHL games, 1,850 points and 33 years of professional hockey. Now you know why they call him "Mr. Hockey."

Did You Know?

When you play passionate hockey for as long as Gordie did, you pick up a few injuries along the way. Here are just some of some of his injuries: a broken wrist, broken toes, torn knee cartilage, broken ribs, a concussion and hundreds of stitches to close countless cuts.

Born: March 31, 1928, in Floral, Saskatchewan
Position: Right Wing
Height: 1.83 m (6')
Weight: 83 kg (205 lbs.)
NHL Teams: Detroit Red Wings, Hartford Whalers

CAREER STATS

Totals 1946–1947 to 1979–1980

	GP	G	A	PTS	PIM
NHL Regular Season	1767	801	1049	1850	1685
WHA Regular Season	419	174	334	508	399
NHL Playoffs	157	68	92	160	220
WHA Playoffs	78	28	43	71	115

Major Awards	
	Stanley Cup: 1950, 1952, 1954, 1955
	Hart Trophy: 1952, 1953, 1957, 1958, 1960, 1963
	Art Ross Trophy: 1951, 1952, 1953, 1954, 1957, 1963

BOBBY HULL

He was fast, tough and had a shot that blazed off the end of his stick like a rocket. Bobby "The Golden Jet" Hull was one of the most captivating players in the NHL.

"There was never a time in my life, that I can remember, where I didn't want to be a professional hockey player," Bobby once said. "It's just all I ever wanted to do — play the game and play it well."

And that he did. During the 1960s and the early 1970s there were few who brought the passion to every shift and every game than Bobby did. It was his passion and magnetism that saw him responsible for the greatest times in the history of not one, but two, professional hockey teams in two different leagues.

> **"Always keep your composure. It's pretty tough to score from the penalty box; and to win, you have to score."**

During the 1950s the Chicago Blackhawks were a struggling team. Season after losing season with no playoff action had fans wondering if things would ever improve. And then came Bobby for the start of the 1957–1958 season. Within four seasons, the Blackhawks were Stanley Cup champions and one of top teams in the league. Bobby spent fifteen seasons with Chicago before he stunned the hockey world in 1972 by leaving to play for the Winnipeg Jets in a brand new league — the World

Hockey Association. The executives of the WHA thought if they could sign a big star like Bobby, the new league might have a chance to be successful. Bobby became the first hockey player in history to be paid one million dollars — an amazing amount of money in 1972.

"At first I thought the offers were kind of a joke," recalled Bobby years later. "I just pretended to go along with it to scare Chicago. Then one day my agent said 'Uh, Bobby, I think these guys are serious.'"

Bobby put the Jets, and the WHA, on the map. In seven seasons with Winnipeg, The Golden Jet scored over 300 goals. Then in 1979 the WHA merged with the NHL. By that time Bobby was near the end of his career. He played a few more games in the NHL with Winnipeg and Hartford before retiring in 1980.

Did You Know?

Along with Chicago teammate Stan Mikita, Bobby popularized the use of the curved stick. Before 1963, all hockey sticks were straight. Mikita accidentally curved the blade of his stick and noticed that when the puck was shot, it behaved unpredictably — like a knuckleball in baseball. Both Mikita and Bobby then started to curve their stick blades on purpose. A new era in stick development had begun.

Born: January 3, 1939, in
Point Anne, Ontario
Position: Left Wing
Height: 1.78 m (5'10")
Weight: 88 kg (195 lbs.)
NHL Teams: Chicago Blackhawks,
Winnipeg Jets, Hartford Whalers

CAREER STATS

Totals 1957–1958 to 1979–1980

	GP	G	A	PTS	PIM
NHL Regular Season	1063	610	560	1170	640
WHA Regular Season	411	303	335	638	183
NHL Playoffs	119	62	67	129	102
WHA Playoffs	60	43	37	80	38

Major Awards	Stanley Cup: 1961
	Hart Trophy: 1965, 1966
	Art Ross Trophy: 1960, 1962, 1966
	Lady Byng Trophy: 1965

GUY LAFLEUR

Guy Lafleur was a natural. His ability to make plays look smooth and spontaneous would bring fans at the Montreal Forum to their feet. He would sail down the ice with his long blond hair trailing behind him as fans chanted his name. For Guy, it was a dream come true.

Growing up in Thurso, Quebec, Guy had idolized the Montreal Canadiens. "We would see them on TV all the time and I used to dream of playing for them one day," said Guy. "My hero was Jean Béliveau."

"Play every game as if it were your last."

His desire to play for the Habs was realized in 1971. Guy was a spectacular junior player with the Quebec Ramparts and led them to a title that year. A few weeks later he was taken first overall by the Canadiens in the NHL Amateur Draft in an unusual deal. At that time the draft was set up so that the worst teams selected first. Montreal was a great team, so they knew the year before that they wouldn't be able to pick Guy — he was expected to be picked first or second. So in 1970 Montreal general manager Sam Pollock made a deal with the California Golden Seals that would give Montreal the first round pick in 1971.

"I was just walking into the room when the first draft pick was announced, and it was me," recalled Guy. "I didn't know what to say. It was my dream to play for Montreal. I was so happy."

Later that year Guy started a spectacular career of 14 seasons with the Habs. During that run he was part of five Stanley Cup Championships. Guy, who was also known as "le Démon Blond" and "The Flower," won the Art Ross Trophy as the top scorer in the NHL three times, and was awarded the Hart Trophy as the NHL's Most Valuable Player twice. He also became the first player in NHL history to score at least 50 goals and record 100 or more points in six consecutive seasons.

Guy retired in 1985, but he just couldn't leave the game. Three years later, still in great shape and still wanting to play, Guy signed with the New York Rangers. The following season he signed as a free agent with the Quebec Nordiques. He played with them for two seasons before finally retiring in 1991.

Did You Know?

Guy would sometimes be in his equipment — with his skates tied up and ready to go — four hours before puck drop! Most NHL players aren't even at the rink that far ahead of time.

Born: September 20, 1951, in Thurso, Quebec	CAREER STATS	Totals 1971–1972 to 1990–1991					
			GP	G	A	PTS	PIM
Position: Right Wing		Regular Season	1126	560	793	1353	399
Height: 1.83 m (6')		Playoffs	128	58	76	134	67
Weight: 84 kg (185 lbs.)		Major Awards	Stanley Cup: 1973, 1976, 1977, 1978, 1979				
NHL Teams: Montreal Canadiens, New York Rangers, Quebec Nordiques			Hart Trophy: 1977, 1978				
			Art Ross Trophy: 1976, 1977, 1978				
			Conn Smythe Trophy: 1977				

MARIO LEMIEUX

How's this for a start to an NHL career: first shift, first possession, first shot and first goal. That's how Mario Lemieux began. As an added bonus, the person he stole the puck from was future Hall of Fame defenseman Ray Bourque.

Mario was taken first overall by the Pittsburgh Penguins in the 1984 NHL Entry Draft. He fit right in with the Penguins and, as a rookie, led the team in scoring with 43 goals and 57 assists. He was only the third rookie ever to earn 100 or more points. He proved himself to be a scoring leader and even surpassed Wayne Gretzky for total points in 1988–1989. Even though the Penguins failed to make the playoffs the first four seasons of Mario's career, the interest that he caused put the team on the map. Fans were finally rewarded with a Cup in 1991, Mario's seventh season with the team.

"He always made me play harder. Mario was such a great player that he made me want to be even better."

— Wayne Gretzky

Then, in 1993 Mario was diagnosed with Hodgkin's disease — a cancer of the lymph nodes. He underwent surgery and radiation treatment. But that didn't stop him. That year he won the Art Ross Trophy with 160 points, despite playing in only 60 games.

Mario had to sit out the entire 1994–1995 season due to his illness and back problems, but came back to win the scoring title the next two seasons.

Following the 1997 season, Mario retired and was fast-tracked into the Hockey Hall of Fame. But three years later, he had a change of heart.

"I wanted my youngest son, Austin, to be able to watch me play," said Mario at the time. And he gave his son plenty to watch as he made his return in the 2000–2001 season, scoring 76 points in only 43 games.

Internationally, Mario led Canada to a gold medal at the 2002 Winter Olympic Games and also helped Canada win the 2004 World Cup of Hockey.

Mario has won the scoring title six times during his career. He also led the Penguins to back-to-back Stanley Cup titles in 1991 and 1992 and was the playoff MVP. Mario won the Calder Trophy in 1985 and has won the Hart Trophy three times. He also won the Cup as a team owner when the Pens captured the Cup in 2009. And he continues to play a role with the team.

As much as Wayne Gretzky was "The Great One," Mario is truly "The Magnificent One."

Did You Know?

On December 31, 1988, Mario scored five goals five different ways in one game — an even-strength goal, a power-play goal, a short-handed goal, a penalty shot and an empty-net goal.

CAREER STATS

Born: October 5, 1965, in Montreal, Quebec
Position: Center / Right Wing
Height: 1.93 m (6'4")
Weight: 102 kg (225 lbs.)
NHL Team: Pittsburgh Penguins

Totals 1984–1985 to 2005–2006

	GP	G	A	PTS	PIM
Regular Season	889	683	1018	1701	818
Playoffs	107	76	96	172	87

Major Awards	Stanley Cup: 1991, 1992
	Hart Trophy: 1988, 1993, 1996
	Calder Trophy: 1985
	Art Ross Trophy: 1988, 1989, 1992, 1993, 1996, 1997
	Conn Smythe Trophy: 1991, 1992

HOWIE MORENZ

There is no doubt that Howie Morenz was the first great superstar of hockey. The 1920s and 1930s was a time when athletes were written and talked about, but only actually watched by a select few — there was no television coverage. His accomplishments became almost mythical.

Howie was playing with a senior team in Stratford, Ontario, when he was only 20 years old, which was pretty unusual at the time. Most often spots on these teams would be taken by older, more experienced local players. He received many offers from professional teams, but he turned them all down until 1923 when the Montreal Canadiens offered him $850 to sign with them and another $2500 for the season. People were shocked. That was a lot of money in 1923 when doctors and lawyers were making a lot less in a year than Howie would make for playing a 24-game hockey season.

"When he realized that he'd never play the game again, he couldn't live with it. I think he died of a broken heart."

— Morenz's teammate Aurele Joliat, talking about his friend's tragic death from a hockey-related injury in 1937

When Howie joined the Canadiens for the 1923–1924 season, he helped lead the team to a Stanley Cup Championship. During his second season with Montreal, Howie scored 27 goals in 30 games, which was amazing at the time. For the next seven seasons the "Stratford Streak" led Montreal in goals and points.

In 1927–1928 he scored a league-high record of 51 points and won the Hart Trophy. He was the biggest sports star in Canada. Fans in Montreal would rise from their seats as Howie flew up the ice.

Howie was a physical player and his small frame took a lot of punishment. Injuries started to take their toll, and his scoring dropped off. In 1934, after 11 seasons with Montreal, Howie was traded. He returned to the Habs in 1936–1937, but his comeback had a sad end. On January 28, 1937, during a home game against Chicago, he was knocked off balance and crashed into the boards where another player hit him. People in the arena could hear the snap as the bones in one of his legs broke. Doctors told him it was unlikely that he would ever skate again.

On March 8, 1937, Howie died due to complications from his injury. More than 10,000 people gathered at the Montreal Forum to pay tribute to one of the greatest hockey stars of their time.

Did You Know?

Howie was one of the first twelve players to be inducted into the Hockey Hall of Fame when it opened in 1945.

Born: June 21, 1902, in
Mitchell, Ontario
Died: March 8, 1937
Position: Center
Height: 1.75 m (5'9")
Weight: 75 kg (165 lbs.)
NHL Teams: Montreal Canadiens,
Chicago Blackhawks, New York Rangers

CAREER STATS

Totals 1923–1924 to 1936–1937

	GP	G	A	PTS	PIM
Regular Season	550	271	201	472	546
Playoffs	39	13	9	22	58
Major Awards	Stanley Cup: 1924, 1930, 1931				
	Hart Trophy: 1928, 1931, 1932				
	Art Ross Trophy: 1928, 1931				

BOBBY ORR

The man who did more than anybody else in his time to change the way the game was played wasn't about style. Bobby Orr was about substance. He was about winning. Style just happened from wanting to be the best.

Bobby set the pace for defensemen. Before him it was a position mainly dominated by bigger, slower players with moderate offensive abilities. Bobby changed all that. His explosive skating and offensive touch made him a playmaker. It showed that a defenseman could be used to create scoring chances, not just stop them. Bobby's approach to the game, as an offensive defenseman, became the model for future defense greats like Denis Potvin, Ray Bourque and Paul Coffey.

"Forget about style, worry about results."

Bobby made his NHL debut on October 19, 1966, against the Detroit Red Wings, when he was just eighteen years old. He impressed the crowd with his defensive plays and even picked up one assist.

"Our fans had heard about this kid for a few years," recalled the Bruins coach at the time, Harry Sinden. "There was a lot of pressure on him, but he met all the expectations. He was a star from the moment they played the national anthem in the opening game of the season."

That season Bobby won the Calder Trophy and was named a Second Team All-Star. That was just the beginning. The following season he won the Norris Trophy — an award he won every year for eight seasons in a row. In 1969–1970 he again won the Norris Trophy, as well as the Hart Trophy, the Art Ross Trophy and the Conn Smythe Trophy — the only player ever to win all four of those awards in the same season. During that spectacular season Bobby also scored the winning goal in overtime to clinch a Stanley Cup Championship for the Bruins.

In the end, Bobby's career was cut short due to chronic knee problems. While he was with the Bruins, he had several major knee surgeries. He left Boston as a free agent and signed with Chicago in 1976. However, he played only 26 games over three seasons with the Blackhawks. After more knee surgery, he finally decided to retire a few games into the 1978–1979 season at the age of 30.

Did You Know?

Bobby Orr was well-known in hockey circles before he was a teenager. Legend has it that a scout from the Boston Bruins organization spotted him when he was 12 years old, playing in a bantam hockey tournament with a team from his hometown of Parry Sound, Ontario. Despite playing against older boys, Bobby was the best player on the ice.

Born: March 20, 1948, in Parry Sound, Ontario
Position: Defense
Height: 1.83 m (6')
Weight: 89 kg (197 lbs.)
NHL Teams: Boston Bruins, Chicago Blackhawks

CAREER STATS

Totals 1966–1967 to 1978–1979

	GP	G	A	PTS	PIM
Regular Season	657	270	645	915	953
Playoffs	74	26	66	92	107

Major Awards Stanley Cup: 1970, 1972
Hart Trophy: 1970, 1971, 1972
Norris Trophy: 1968, 1969, 1970, 1971, 1972, 1973, 1974, 1975
Calder Trophy: 1967
Art Ross Trophy: 1970, 1975
Conn Smythe Trophy: 1970, 1972

JACQUES PLANTE

Jacques "Jake the Snake" Plante was more than just one of the greatest goaltenders ever — he was a man who forever changed the way the position was played.

Born in Shawinigan Falls, Quebec, Jacques played with a local team before leaving for Quebec City to tend goal with the junior hockey Quebec Citadelles. Only two years later, he made his debut with the Montreal Canadiens. It was in a thrilling first-round Stanley Cup playoff series in 1953 against the Chicago Blackhawks. Heading into game six, Montreal was facing elimination. Jacques started the game and shut Chicago out 3–0. He started the next game and Montreal defeated the Hawks 4–1 to win the series. Although Jacques started the first two games in the final, he stepped aside for veteran goalie Gerry McNeil. He went on to play 112 games in the Stanley Cup playoffs in 18 seasons — an NHL record 25 of those games in the final.

"I was so nervous that I couldn't even tie up my skates."

— Jacques Plante recalls starting his first game with the Montreal Canadiens during the 1953 Stanley Cup playoffs

---

Jacques was the first goalie to perfect the now common practice of coming away from his net to play the puck. Today goalies do this all the time. But before Plante, goalies hardly ever went behind the goal to stop or pass a puck.

But his biggest contribution to the game has to be the introduction of the goalie mask. He was wearing one in practice as far back as 1956, but his coach told him that he would never be allowed to wear it during a game. That all changed on November 2, 1959, when the Canadiens were in New York to play the Rangers. Jacques was hit in the face by a shot and had to leave the ice for 20 minutes to get stitched up. He returned wearing his mask. The coach agreed to allow Jacques to wear the mask only until his cuts had healed. However, Jacques never went back to playing without one. Within a few seasons most goalies in the league followed his lead.

Jacques played on six Stanley Cup-winning teams and won the Vezina Trophy as the top goalie in the NHL seven times. He played into his early 40s before retiring in 1975 after a final season in the World Hockey Association. He died of cancer in 1986 at the age of 57.

Did You Know?

Despite having his name on the Stanley Cup six times, Jacques holds the distinction of having it misspelled FIVE times! There are actually a number of spelling mistakes on the Cup.

CAREER STATS

Born: January 17, 1929, in
Shawinigan Falls, Quebec
Died: February 26, 1986
Position: Goaltender
Height: 1.83 m (6')
Weight: 79 kg (175 lbs.)
NHL Teams: Montreal Canadiens,
New York Rangers, St. Louis Blues,
Toronto Maple Leafs, Boston Bruins

Totals 1952–1953 to 1972–1973

	GP	W	L	T	SO	GAA
Regular Season	837	437	246	145	82	2.38
Playoffs	112	71	37	—	14	2.14

Major Awards	Stanley Cup: 1953, 1956, 1957, 1958, 1959, 1960
	Vezina Trophy: 1956, 1957, 1958, 1959, 1960, 1962, 1969
	Hart Trophy: 1962

DENIS POTVIN

More than any other player in the history of the franchise, Denis Potvin symbolizes the New York Islanders. The team was only two years old when he was drafted, first overall in 1973. General manager Bill Torrey thought the young defenseman would be perfect to help build a championship team. He was right. The Islanders went from being a young, struggling expansion franchise to a dynasty that won four Stanley Cup Championships in a row and made five straight trips to the final.

"It was a great time in the game," Denis said, reflecting back to those years. "It was a time when teams could hold on to guys and develop them. You had the ability to really become a team."

"I've been asked before which Cup meant the most to me and I'll usually tell people that it's like having four kids. Which one do you love the most? They are all different, but maybe the first one is special because it's the first one."

Denis quickly developed into a first-rate defenseman. In his first NHL season he had 17 goals and 37 assists, and won the Calder Trophy. Denis also showed a lot of toughness for a 20-year-old, refusing to back down from many of the older players who often tried to intimidate rookies.

Although Denis was known for his scoring ability while in junior hockey, he knew that to be a great defenseman in the NHL you have to be able to defend as well as score. He learned this part of the game from his coach, long-time NHL defenseman Al Arbour.

"Al taught me that, to be the best, you had to take responsibility for what went on in both ends of the rink," said Denis.

Finally, in the 1979–1980 season, it all came together for the Isles. After missing most of the season with a thumb injury, Denis returned in time for the playoffs and helped New York defeat a tough Philadelphia team in six games. It was the first of four consecutive championships for the Islanders.

Denis ended his 15-season career in 1987–1988 with 1,052 points in 1,060 regular season games. He was the first defenseman in the history of the NHL to hit the 1000 career-point mark. Denis was inducted into the Hockey Hall of Fame in 1991.

Did You Know?

Denis has had his number retired by not one, but two, teams. Both his junior team, the Ottawa 67's, and the Islanders have the number 5 displayed in the rafters of their home rink.

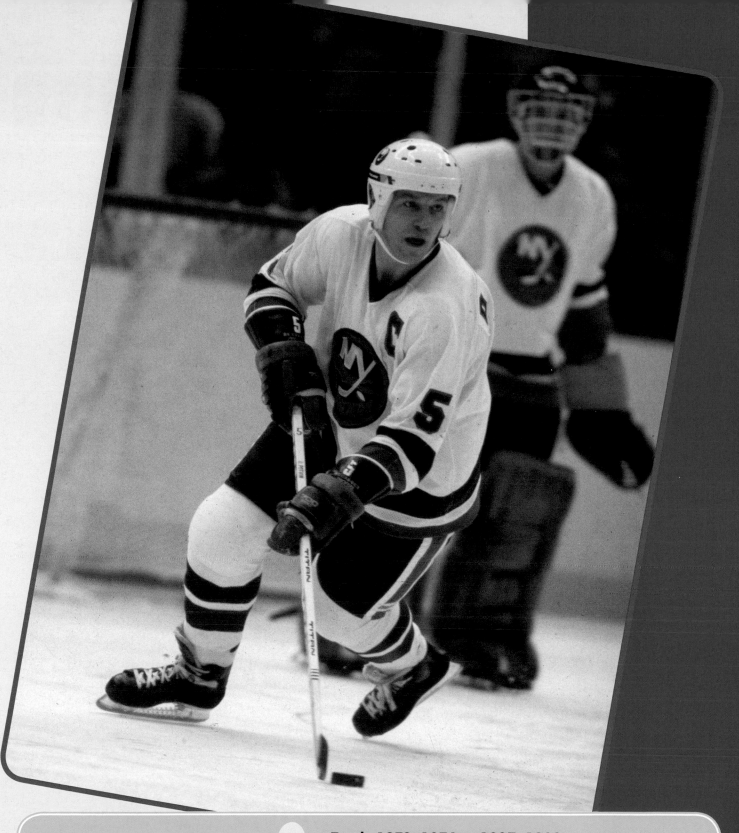

CAREER STATS

Born: October 29, 1953, in Ottawa, Ontario
Position: Defense
Height: 1.83 m (6')
Weight: 83 kg (205 lbs.)
NHL Team: New York Islanders

Totals 1973–1974 to 1987–1988

	GP	G	A	PTS	PIM
Regular Season	1060	310	742	1052	1354
Playoffs	185	56	108	164	253

Major Awards	Stanley Cup: 1980, 1981, 1982, 1983
	Calder Trophy: 1974
	Norris Trophy: 1976, 1978, 1979

Take a look at almost any photo of Maurice "The Rocket" Richard from his early days in the NHL and you can't help but notice his eyes: the fierce determination and the focus on winning whenever he put on the sacred *bleu, blanc et rouge* of the Montreal Canadiens.

Maurice had suffered wrist and ankle injuries playing junior and senior hockey, so he was regarded as small and fragile when he entered the NHL. In his first year with the Habs he suffered a broken ankle. His coach, Dick Irvin, said: "Richard may just be too brittle to play in the National Hockey League." Even Maurice was worried about suffering three big injuries in three seasons. He didn't want to develop a reputation as an injury-prone player.

"His eyes were terrifying. When he was roaring towards me with the puck they would sparkle, crackle like a pinball machine."

— Hall of Fame goalie Glenn Hall, talking about playing against Richard back in the 1950s

---

During training camp the following year, The Rocket was put on a line with a couple of veteran players: Elmer Lach and Toe Blake. The three were a perfect match for one another and the "Punch Line" was born. Richard caught fire, scoring 32 goals and helping lead Montreal to a first-place finish and a Stanley Cup Championship.

The most infamous story in Maurice's career happened late in the 1954–1955 season. During a game in Boston on March 13, 1955, Maurice's legendary temper got the better of him after a Bruins player elbowed him from behind. He got into a fight and was kicked out of the game. NHL President Clarence Campbell later suspended Maurice for the rest of the season and the playoffs. Montreal fans were outraged. When Campbell showed up at the Montreal Forum for a game on March 17, he was pelted with eggs and attacked by a fan. The crowd went crazy, and the game was forfeited to Detroit as police tried to clear the building.

Although many of his records have since been broken, The Rocket was first to score 50 goals in 50 games and only the second to score five goals in a playoff game. He was the first to record eight points in a single game and to reach 500 career goals.

Maurice was more than just a hockey player: he was, and is, a cultural icon. When he died in 2000, his funeral was broadcast across Canada.

Did You Know?

No one is absolutely certain where the famous nickname "Rocket" came from. Some say it came from one of his teammates, and others seem to recall that the nickname first appeared in the pages of the Montreal Gazette.

Born: August 4, 1921, in Montreal,
Quebec
Died: May 27, 2000
Position: Right Wing
Height: 1.78 m (5'10")
Weight: 77 kg (170 lbs.)
NHL Team: Montreal Canadiens

CAREER STATS

Totals 1942–1943 to 1959–1960

	GP	G	A	PTS	PIM
Regular Season	978	544	421	965	1285
Playoffs	133	82	44	126	188

Major Awards	Stanley Cup: 1944, 1946, 1953, 1956, 1957, 1958, 1959, 1960
	Hart Trophy: 1947

PATRICK ROY

Without a doubt, Patrick Roy was the greatest goalie of his era. He finished a brilliant 18-season career with more regular season wins and playoff wins than any other goalie in NHL history. He won the Stanley Cup four times — twice with Montreal and twice with Colorado — and is the only goalie in NHL history to win more than 200 regular-season games with two different teams.

Patrick was the first of a great wave of NHL goalies to come out of the Quebec Junior League playing the butterfly style of goal. Although popular now, back when Patrick entered the NHL, most goalies still used the more traditional stand up style.

"I lived a dream and had fun for more than 18 years playing a game I love."

— Patrick Roy, talking about his retirement

As much as Patrick was renowned for his talent, he was also known for a competitive streak that occasionally got the better of him.

"He might have been the only goalie I ever coached who was truly the leader of his team," recalled Jacques Demers, who was the coach with Montreal when Patrick won his second Stanley Cup in 1993. "He was the most intense player I ever coached. He absolutely hated to lose."

The most famous example of Patrick's hot temper came in what turned out to be his final game with the Montreal Canadiens. On December 2, 1995,

Montreal was playing at home against the Detroit Red Wings. It was one of the worst home games in Canadiens' history. Patrick fumed as the team struggled. He had already given up eight goals by the second period. His coach, Mario Tremblay, wasn't helping him by keeping him in net. He wanted to be pulled. Usually when this happens, a coach will make a goaltending change. After giving up his ninth goal, Patrick had had enough. He skated over to team president Ronald Corey and told him that he "had played his last game for the Montreal Canadiens." A few days later he was traded to Colorado, and a few months later he was celebrating a Stanley Cup Championship with his new team.

Like many great players, Patrick wanted to walk away while he was still one of the best. In 2003, following yet another 30-plus win season (the record-setting 13th of his career), Patrick called it quits. One of the greatest careers in sports had come to a close.

Did You Know?

Like many goalies, Patrick was highly superstitious. He tried not to touch the red or blue lines and also talked to his goal posts. Patrick, unlike most goalies, was also famous for "trash talking" opposition shooters after he'd robbed them with a big save.

Born: October 5, 1965, in Quebec City, Quebec	CAREER STATS	Totals 1984–1985 to 2002–2003						
Position: Goaltender			GP	W	L	T	SO	GAA
Height: 1.88 m (6'2")		Regular Season	1029	551	315	131	66	2.54
Weight: 84 kg (185 lbs.)		Playoffs	247	151	94	—	23	2.30
NHL Teams: Montreal Canadiens, Colorado Avalanche		Major Awards	Stanley Cup: 1986, 1993, 1996, 2001					
			Vezina Trophy: 1989, 1990, 1992					
			Conn Smythe Trophy: 1986, 1993, 2001					

DARRYL SITTLER

Darryl Sittler averaged more than a point per game during a fifteen-season career with three different NHL teams. He was a talented offensive player and the captain of one of the most celebrated franchises in hockey — the Toronto Maple Leafs. On the international stage, he scored the winning goal for Canada in the first Canada Cup in 1976, making him a national hero.

Heading into the 1975–1976 season, Darryl was named the second-youngest captain in the history of the Leafs. He was only 24 years old, but already entering his sixth NHL season. At that time the Leafs were a struggling team — but Darryl was considered one of the bright lights of the franchise and the league. Becoming the team's captain seemed to propel Darryl to even greater heights. He led the Leafs that year with 100 points — the first Leaf ever to do so.

"It was truly an outstanding performance."

— a Toronto newspaper report following Darryl Sittler's NHL record 10 points in a single game

---

Then on February 7, 1976, the Leafs faced the Boston Bruins, one of the top teams in the NHL. It was a game that would be a defining moment in Darryl's career. "I remember that the Bruins were a very good team," recalled Darryl years later. "They had traded Phil Esposito earlier that season and picked up Brad Park and Jean Ratelle and were playing really well."

But that didn't matter. Darryl set up two goals in the first period. In the second he scored three goals and got two more assists. Quite a night, seven points in two periods, but he wasn't finished. He added a hat trick in the third period for a total of 10 points — an NHL single-game record that stands to this day.

Later that season Darryl went on to tie an NHL single-game playoff record when he scored five goals. That September he scored the championship-winning goal for Team Canada — in overtime — against Czechoslovakia in the first Canada Cup international hockey tournament.

After playing for the Philadelphia Flyers and the Detroit Red Wings for a few seasons, Darryl retired in 1985. He was inducted into the Hockey Hall of Fame in 1989. But Darryl never could leave the Leafs. In 1991 he returned to work in the club's marketing and public relations office.

Did You Know?

In the 1976 Canada Cup tournament, the man who gave Darryl the tip on how to beat Czech goalie Vladimir Dzurilla in overtime — "fake a slapper, if the goalie comes out draw it back in and go wide and deeper" — was none other than Canadian assistant coach, and now iconic television personality, Don Cherry.

Born: September 18, 1950, in
Kitchener, Ontario
Position: Center / Left Wing
Height: 1.83 m (6')
Weight: 86 kg (190 lbs.)
NHL Teams: Toronto Maple
Leafs, Philadelphia Flyers,
Detroit Red Wings

CAREER STATS

Totals 1970–1971 to 1984–1985

	GP	G	A	PTS	PIM
Regular Season	1096	484	637	1121	948
Playoffs	76	29	45	74	137

MAJOR NHL AWARDS AND TOP WINNERS

Lady Byng Memorial Trophy

Awarded to the player judged to have exhibited the best sportsmanship combined with a high standard of playing ability. Selected by the Professional Hockey Writers' Association.

Named after Lady Byng, who was the wife of Canada's then Governor General. First awarded in 1924–1925.

Top winners: Frank Boucher (7), Wayne Gretzky (5), *Pavel Datsyuk, Red Kelly (4)

Conn Smythe Trophy

Awarded to the player most valuable to his team in the Stanley Cup Playoffs. Selected by the Professional Hockey Writers' Asscociation.

Named after Conn Smythe, a coach, general manager and owner of the Toronto Maple Leafs. First awarded after the 1964–1965 playoffs.

Top winners: Patrick Roy (3), Wayne Gretzky, Mario Lemieux, Bobby Orr, Bernie Parent (2)

Hart Memorial Trophy

Awarded to the player judged to be the most valuable to his team. Selected by the Professional Hockey Writers' Association.

Named after Dr. David Hart, the father of Cecil Hart, former coach and manager of the Montreal Canadiens. First awarded in 1923–1924.

Top winners: Wayne Gretzky (9), Gordie Howe (6), Eddie Shore (4)

James Norris Memorial Trophy

Awarded to the defense player who demonstrates throughout his season the greatest all-round ability. Selected by the Professional Hockey Writers' Association.

Named after James Norris, who purchased the Detroit franchise in 1932 and renamed it the Red Wings. First awarded in 1953–1954.

Top winners: Bobby Orr (8), Doug Harvey (7), *Nicklas Lidstrom, Ray Bourque (5)

Art Ross Trophy

Awarded to the player who leads the league in scoring points at the end of the regular season.

Named after Art Ross, an executive with the Boston Bruins and a member of the Hockey Hall of Fame. First awarded in 1947–1948.

Top winners: Wayne Gretzky (10), Gordie Howe, Mario Lemieux (6), Phil Esposito, Jaromir Jagr (5)

Vezina Trophy

Awarded to the goalkeeper judged to be the best. Selected by the NHL general managers.

Named in memory of outstanding Canadiens goalie Georges Vezina who collapsed during an NHL game in 1925 and died of tuberculosis a few months later. First awarded in 1926–1927.

Top winners: Jacques Plante (7), Bill Durnan, Dominik Hasek (6)

*active player

NHL RECORDS

Top 10 All-Time Goal-Scoring Leaders

1. Wayne Gretzky	894
2. Gordie Howe	801
3. Brett Hull	741
4. Marcel Dionne	731
5. Phil Esposito	717
6. Mike Gartner	708
7. Mark Messier	694
8. Steve Yzerman	692
9. Mario Lemieux	690
10. Luc Robitaille	668

Top 10 All-Time Shutout Leaders

1. Martin Brodeur*	116
2. Terry Sawchuk	103
3. George Hainsworth	94
4. Glenn Hall	84
5. Jacques Plante	82
6. Alec Connell	81
7. Tiny Thompson	81
8. Dominik Hasek	81
9. Tony Esposito	76
10. Ed Belfour	76

Top 10 All-Time Point Leaders

1. Wayne Gretzky	2857
2. Mark Messier	1887
3. Gordie Howe	1850
4. Ron Francis	1798
5. Marcel Dionne	1771
6. Steve Yzerman	1755
7. Mario Lemieux	1723
8. Joe Sakic	1641
9. Jaromir Jagr	1599
10. Phil Esposito	1590

Top 10 All-Time Win Leaders

1. Martin Brodeur*	625
2. Patrick Roy	551
3. Ed Belfour	484
4. Curtis Joseph	454
5. Terry Sawchuk	447
6. Jacques Plante	437
7. Tony Esposito	423
8. Glenn Hall	407
9. Grant Fuhr	403
10. Chris Osgood *	401

(*active player)

Teams with the most
Stanley Cups

1.	Montreal	23	10.	New Jersey	3
2.	Toronto	13	11.	Philadelphia	2
3.	Detroit	11	12.	Colorado	2
4.	Boston	5	13.	Dallas	1
5.	Edmonton	5	14.	Calgary	1
6.	Chicago	4	15.	Carolina	1
7.	New York Rangers	4	16.	Anaheim	1
8.	New York Islanders	4	17.	Tampa Bay	1
9.	Pittsburgh	3			

(All other teams have never won the Stanley Cup.)

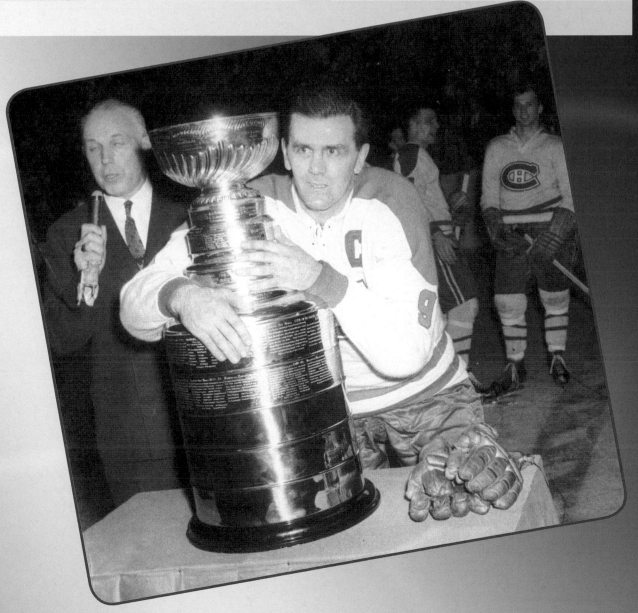

WHO ARE YOUR ALL-TIME GREATS?

Center:

_____
_____
_____
_____
_____
_____

Defense:

_____
_____
_____
_____
_____
_____

Right Wing:

_____
_____
_____
_____
_____
_____

Goal:

_____
_____
_____
_____
_____

Left Wing:

_____
_____
_____
_____
_____
_____